W9-AYV-180

MELODIA

A COMPREHENSIVE COURSE IN

SIGHT-SINGING

(SOLFEGGIO)

THE EDUCATIONAL PLAN BY

SAMUEL W. COLE

THE EXERCISES WRITTEN AND SELECTED BY

LEO R. LEWIS

OLIVER DITSON COMPANY

Theodore Presser Company, Sole Representative

588 No. Gulph Road · King of Prussia, PA 19406

www.presser.com

MADE IN U. S. A.

INTRODUCTORY

The Value of Sight-Singing

For at least two centuries training in sight-singing has been recognized in Europe as fundamental to all technical education in music. Americans have seemed to set little store by such training; for, today, the great majority of our professional musicians, not only instrumentalists but also vocalists, need unerring instrumental support in " singing at sight " a part-song or an anthem which has modulations to any except closely related keys, or which abounds in the larger intervals. Obviously, inability to read at sight does not preclude good performance, after familiarity has been gained by instrumental assistance; but probably no one would deny that the possibilities of artistic achievement are infinitely greater when one has acquired the confidence born of genuine ability to sing at sight — which ability may be defined as the power to know the units of rhythm and of relative pitch of any rational musical phrase, and to prove that knowledge by singing it correctly at first sight.

Much Material is Necessary

Many works on sight-singing have been compiled and written for use in the public schools. But the authors of Melodia believe that there is need of more and better graded material for use in conservatories and by private teachers. The present work is an attempt to meet this need. It represents the results of many years' experience, and is based on the belief that, whatever be the method of presenting the elements of the subject, the surest road to growth is through actual performance of a great number of carefully graded tasks.

Confidence Must be Developed

A second fundamental thought has been that a high degree of self-confidence must be developed before one can " stand up and sing " alone at sight a somewhat difficult musical phrase, without other assistance than the sounding of the key-note. Experience has shown that rhythmical problems are quite as often stumbling-blocks to musical students as are tonal problems. Therefore, in Melodia, the first eighty pages, which are written without skips primarily to develop a ready confidence, contain many and varied examples of each of the conventional rhythm-forms; and the most deliberate progressiveness is maintained in the introduction of new difficulties. In a word, it is a feature of Melodia that early emphasis is laid upon rhythmical problems.

The Treatment of Large Intervals

In the treatment of the larger intervals there is also a departure from the conventional procedure. Instead of taking them in the order of small to great, the octave is first presented, because experience shows that it is the only " skip " definitely recognized as such by most beginners. The sevenths, sixths, etc., are then presented both in their relation to the octave and as composites of the steps and half-steps with which the student is already thoroughly familiar.

General Features of Melodia

A glance at the headings of the successive Series will indicate in detail the comprehensiveness of the plan. The following general points may be noted:

1, The typographical arrangement is such that a very large amount of material is brought within comparatively narrow limits;

2, The normal compass of *average* voices (an octave and five notes from low A) is seldom exceeded;

3, Nearly one-half of the unison exercises are written in the bass clef, thus forcing sopranos and altos to become familiar with that clef;

4, The two-part exercises are all written so that they may be inverted, the bass being made the tune, and the tune the bass; or they may be sung by male voices only or by female voices only; thus, each two-part page represents two pages of practice material;

5, Again, the two-part exercises are adapted to use by teacher with pupil in private vocal lessons;

6, Since all indications of phrasing are lacking, opportunity is offered for constructive work of the highest educational value.

Individual Work Essential

It is expected that, even when the book is studied in large classes, much work in individual reading will be required by the Instructor; for, after all, no one has fully mastered sight-singing who cannot sing alone, while beating time after the conventional forms.

As a special—and, perhaps, novel—help in developing the sense of individual independence in ensemble, there have been included, in Series I, exercises which may be sung simultaneously. Cases of this sort are indicated in connection with each of the respective exercises. Thus I 233 may be sung with I 243, I 246 with I 263, etc. Some teachers believe so fully in this method of developing independence that they cause exercises in the same key, and with the same number of measures, to be sung together, without regard to the tone-content of the exercises. This practice, artistically unjustifiable, may have, in moderate use, educational value.

The Goal of Melodia

Melodia undertakes to prepare students to meet the most difficult tasks in pitch and rhythm set by masters of choral composition. If suggestions of phrases from some of the masters have occasionally been incorporated in the original exercises, the reader may be willing to waive a charge of unjustifiable appropriation, in view of the specific object of the whole work.

The Modulatory Studies

Pages 76 to 80 contain Modulatory Exercises, some of which may well be studied earlier than their position in the book would indicate. The relationship between the objective keys and the tonic is indicated by Roman numerals,—capitals for major keys and small capitals for minor keys. Thus, "To ii" means that the exercise illustrates modulation to the minor key based on its super-tonic of the prevailing scale—to D minor, if the piece is in C major. Such an exercise may well be studied in connection with any earlier exercise which modulates to any similarly related key—to F-sharp minor from E major, for instance. Reference to these exercises is occasionally made in the earlier pages of Series IV: but the teacher may best judge whether more detailed study of key-relationship is desirable.

Matters of Notation.

There has been no attempt to preserve absolute uniformity as to the details of notation throughout the book. On the contrary, it has been deemed wise to present a variety of forms and usages, in order to accustom the student to the practices of various authors and editors.

A word is necessary as to the insertion of clefs and the use of bars, which features, on casual view, might appear to be unsystematic and needlessly unconventional. As a matter of fact, considerations of brevity have prompted several departures from the established usage. For the guidance of the singer, however, but a single direction is necessary: **the prevailing key-signature and time-signature are not cancelled unless a clef or the regular double-bar [‖] is inserted.** The double-thin-bar [||] is therefore not to be regarded as necessitating a new indication of key or time. The time-signature may change while the key-signature remains. The regular double-bar appears where either a clef or a *key*-signature is changed. The meaning of the single-thick-bar [**|**] or the double-thick-bar [**||**], as in the Modulatory Exercises and in connection with repeat-signs, is, in the respective cases, obvious.

THE SOURCES OF THE SELECTED EXERCISES

The authorship of the selected exercises and of the excerpts, is indicated by letters following the respective numbers. An asterisk shows that some modification other than transposition has been made, but not such as to impair the original character. Below is a key to the indications of the letters. All exercises not so marked have been written for this book.

Ad T. Anderton [1836-]
Ab D. F. E. Auber [1782-1871]
Bh J. S. Bach [1685-1750]
Be L. van Beethoven [1770-1827]
Bt A. Bertalotti [1665-1730(?)]
Bn H. Bönicke [1821-1879]
Br J. Brahms [1833-1897]
Cl G. Carulli [1800-1877]
Cb E. Chabrier [1842-1894]
Ck G. W. Chadwick [1854-]
Ch L. Cherubini [1760-1842]
Cn P. Cornelius [1824-1874]
Du F. Durante [1684-1755]
Fi C. H. Fischer [1800-1875(?)]
Fr C. Franck [1822-1890]

Gn C. F. Gounod [1818-1893]
Hd G. F. Händel [1685-1759]
Hr H. L. Hasler [1564-1612]
Hs J. A. Hasse [1699-1783]
Hn J. Haydn [1732-1809]
Hg J. Higgs [1829-1902]
Kb J. P. Kirnberger [1721-1783]
La H. F. Langlé [1741-1807]
Ls O. Lasso [1532-1594]
Lm H. Lemoine [1786-1854]
Lo L. Leo [1694-1756]
Lw C Löwe [1796-1869]
Mn F. Mendelssohn [1809-1847]
Mi J. Minard [1845(?)-]
Mz W. A. Mozart [1756-1791]

Na J. Nares [1715-1783]
Pa A. Panseron [1796-1859]
Py C. H. H. Parry [1848-]
Rd J. J. Rodolphe [1730-1812]
Rs G. Rossini [1792-1868]
Sb J. N. Schelble [1789-1837]
Sn F. Schneider [1786-1853]
Sm R. Schumann [1810-1856]
St J. A. Steffani [1726-1800(?)]
Ts W. Tschirch [1818-1892]
Vd G. Verdi [1813-1901]
Wg R. Wagner [1813-1883]
Wb S. Webbe [1740-1816]
Wn B. Widmann [1820-]
Wll F. Wüllner [1832-1902]

TABLE OF CONTENTS

INTRODUCTORY v

BOOK I

FIRST SERIES 1

One-part diatonic exercises in step-wise melody — G and F clefs — All major keys to B and to D-flat inclusive — All representations of notes and rests of whole-beat length and multiples thereof — Elementary presentation of the divided beat.

SECOND SERIES 21

Two-part diatonic exercises in step-wise melody — Keys to B and to D-flat inclusive — All representations of notes as in First Series, with greater variety and length of rests — The divided beat in fuller presentation.

BOOK II

THIRD SERIES 41

One-part exercises in step-wise melody in all keys — Graded presentation of all chromatic tones, except flat-2 and flat-5 — Development of the minor — The dotted note involving division of the beat — Triple and quadruple division of the beat.

FOURTH SERIES 61

Two-part exercises in step-wise melody in all keys — Chromatic tones, modulatory and ornamental — Development of incidental and extended modulation — Syncopation — Mingling of double and triple divisions of the beat.

FIFTH SERIES 81

One-part exercises — Systematic treatment of intervals, beginning with the larger — Skips to and from chromatic tones having obvious key-relationship —The commoner augmented and diminished intervals.

BOOK III

SIXTH SERIES 101

Two-part exercises embodying all intervals treated in Fifth Series — More elaborate development of rhythmical difficulties, especially of syncopation — Lengthy solfeggi from German, French, and English sources — Canon and Fugue.

SEVENTH SERIES 131

One-part exercises — Systematic treatment of skips to, from, and between chromatic tones — Introductory study of passages whose chromatics "deny" the signature — Advanced solfeggi from foreign sources — Specimen difficulties, without text, from the classics.

EIGHTH SERIES 151

Two-part exercises, involving all the difficulties treated in Seventh Series, and fully reviewing the rhythmical problems earlier treated — Maximum difficulties of mediated modulation — Special studies in the development of independence of the parts.

BOOK IV

NINTH SERIES 161

One-part exercises — Typical passages from early and recent composers, with text, of difficulty ranging from medium to great — Full exposition of chromatics which "deny" the signature — Arbitrary changes of tonality.

TENTH SERIES 177

Two-part exercises, with text — Representative excerpts from early and recent composers, with a few new exercises, embodying maximum difficulties of pitch and rhythm, as well as the utmost independence of parts.

ELEVENTH SERIES 191

Two-part exercises, partly without and partly with text, in the following Church Modes: Æolian, Dorian, Jonian, Mixolydian, Phrygian — Canonic imitation, strict and free, in other intervals than that of the octave.

MELODIA - BOOK I

FIRST SERIES

One-part diatonic exercises in step-wise melody — G and F clefs — All major keys to B and D-flat inclusive — All representations of notes and rests of whole-beat length and mnltiples thereof — Elementary presentation of the divided beat

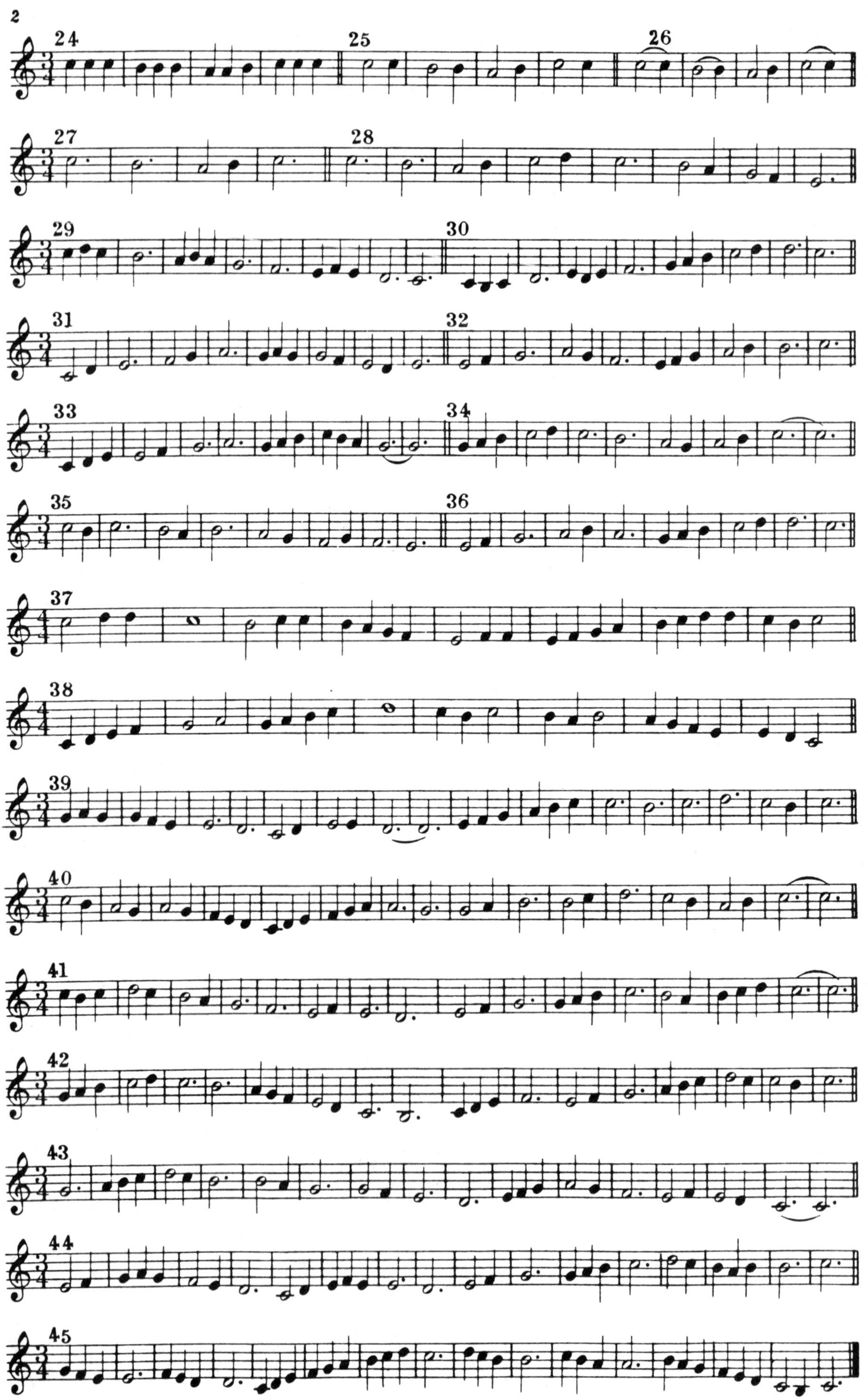

5-57-67645-200

46
47
48
49
50
51
52
53
54
55
56
57
58
59
60
61
62
63
64
65
66
67
68
69
70
71
72
73
74
75

76

77

78

79

80

81

82

83

84

85

86

87

88

89

90

91

92

93

5-57-67645-200

94
95
96
97
98
99
100
101
102
103
104
105
106
107
108

109
110
111
112
113
114
115
116
117
118
119
120
121
122
123
124
125
126
127

128

129

130

131

132

133

134

135

136

137

138

139

140

141

142

143

144

145

146

147

5-57-67645-200

148

149

150

151

152

153

154

155

156

157

158

159

160

161

162

163

164

165

166

167

5-57-67645-200

168

169

170

171

172

173

174

175

176

177

178

179

180

181

182

183

184

185

186

187

188
189
190
191
192
193
194
195
196
197
198
199
200
201
202
203
204
205

All Unison Bass Exercises are to be sung by all singers, the Sopranos and Altos sounding, of course, an octave higher.

206

207

208

209

210

211

212

213

214

215

216

217

218

219

220

221

222

223

224

225

226
227
228
229
230
231
232
233 (with 243)
234(with 244)
235
236
237
238
239
240
241
242
243(with 233)
244(with 234)
245

246 (with 263)
247
248
249 (with 264)
250
251
252
253
254
255
256
257
258
259
260
261
262
263 (with 246)
264 (with 249)
265

266
267
268 (with 279)
269
270
271
272
273
274
275
276
277
278
279 (with 268)
280
281

282
283
284
285
286
287
288
289
290
291 (with 300)
292
293
294
295
296
297
298
299
300 (with 291)
301
302
303

304
305
306
307 (with 312)
308
309
310
311
312 (with 307)
313
314
315
316
317

318
319
320
321 (with 338)
322 (with 337)
323
324
325
326
327
328 (with 339 or 340)
329
330
331
332
333
334
335
336
337 (with 322)
338(with 321)
339 (with 328)
340 (with 328)
341
342
343

344
345
346
347
348
349
350
351
352
353
354
355
356
357
358
359
360
361 (with 378)
362
363
364 (with 379)
365
366
367
368
369
370
371
372
373
374
375
376
377
378 (with 361)
379 (with 364)
380

5-57-67645-200

5-57-67645-200

SECOND SERIES

Two-part diatonic exercises in step-wise melody — Keys to B and to D-flat inclusive — All representations of notes as in Series I, with greater variety and length of rests — The divided beat in fuller presentation

12 Wn

13 Wn

14 Wn

15 Wn

16 Wn

17 Wn

18 (Compare with 10)

19 Wn

20 Wn

21 Wn

22 Wn
23
24
25
26
27
28
29
30

31
32
33
34
35
36
37

38
39
40
41
42
43
44

45
46
47
48
49
50

51
52
53
54
55
56

57

58

59

60

61

62

63

64

65

66

67

68
69
70
71
72
73
74

75
76
77
78
79

80
81
82
83
84

85
86
87
88

89
90
91

92
93
94
95
96
97

98
99
100
101
102
103

104

105

106

107

108

109

110

111

5-57-67645-200

112
113
114
115

116
117
118
119

MELODIA - BOOK II

THIRD SERIES

One-part exercises in step-wise melody in all keys — Graded presentation of all chromatic tones, except ♭2 and ♭5 — Development of the minor — The dotted note involving division of the beat — Triple and quadruple division of the beat

13

14

15

16

17

18

19

20

21

22

23

24

25

26

27

5-57-67645-200

28
29
30
31
32
33
34
35
36
37
38

39
40
41
42
43
44
45
46
47
48
49
50
51
52
53

54
55
56
57
58
59
60
61
62
63
64

65
66
67
68
69
70
71
72
73
74

75
76
77
78
79
80
81
82
83
84
85
86
87
88

89
90
91
92
93
94
95
96
97
98
99
100
101
102
103
104
105
106

107
108
109
110
111
112
113
114
115
116
117
118
119
120

121
122
123
124
125
126
126a
127
128
129
130
131
132
133
134
135
136
137

138
139
140
141
142
143
144
145
146
147
148
149
150
151
152
153
154

155
156
157
158
159
160
161
162
163
164
165
166

167
168
169
170
171
172
173
174
175
176

177
178
179
180
181
182
183
184
185
186
187
188
189
190
191
192
193
194
195
196
197
198

199 (Compare 197-8)
200 (Compare 187)
201
202
203
204
205
206
207
208
209
210

211 (Compare 197-8 and 199)
212 (Compare 187 and 200)
213
214
215
216
217
218
219
220
221

222
223
224
225
226
227(Compare 223)
228
229

230
231
232
233
234
235
236
237
238(Compare 237)
239

240
241
242
243 (Compare 204)
244 (Compare 205)
245
246
247

5-57-67645-200

FOURTH SERIES

Two-part exercises in step-wise melody in all keys — Chromatic tones, modulatory and ornamental — Development of incidental and extended modulation — Syncopation — Mingling of double and triple divisions of the beat

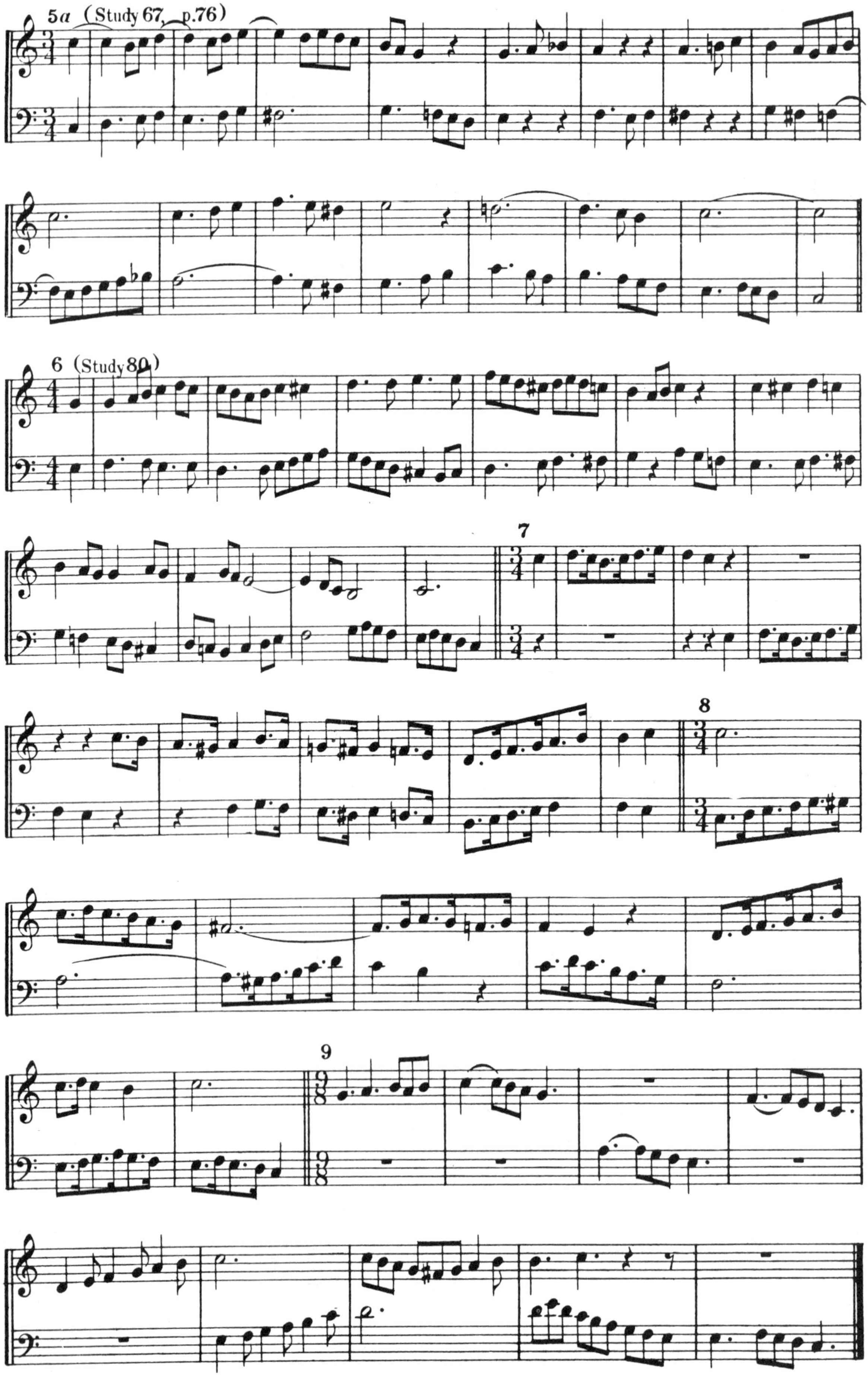

5a (Study 67, p.76)

6 (Study 80)

7

8

9

10 (Study 73)

11

12

13

14

5-57-67645-200

15
16
17
18
19
20

21
22
23 (Study 70)
24

25
26
27
28
29
30

31

32

33

34

35

5-57-67645-200

36
37
38
39
40

41
42
43
44

45
46
47
48
49

50
51
52

53 (Study 78)
54(Compare III, 208)
55

56 (Compare III, 233)
57

58
59
60
61
62
63

64 (Study 80, 81, 82)
65
66

MODULATORY EXERCISES.

* For explanation of the Roman numerals, see the Preface

5-57-67645-200

74 To V and I, and suggesting IV.
75 Compare 74
76 Suggesting II, III, and V.
77 Compare 76
78 To VI via II (II) and III (III).
79 Compare 78
80 To II twice.

81 To remoter keys.
82

83
84

85

FIFTH SERIES

One-part exercises — Systematic treatment of intervals, beginning with the larger — **Skips to and from** chromatic tones having obvious key-relationship — The commoner augmented and diminished intervals

19
20
21
22
23
24
25
26
27
28
29
30
31
32
33
34
35
36
37
38
39
40

41
42
43
44
45
46
47
48
49
50
51
52
53
54
55
56
57
58
59
60

61
62
63
64
65
66
67
68
69
70
71
72

73
74
75
76
77
78
79
80
81
82
83
84
85
86
87
88
89
90

5-57-67645-200

111
112
113
114
115
116
117
118
119
120
121
122
123
124

125
126
127
128
129
130
131
132
133
134
135
136
137
138

139
140
141
142
143
144
145
146
147
148
149
150
151
152
153
154
155
156
157

158
159
160
161
162
163
164
165
166
167
168
169
170
171

172

173

174

175

176

177

178

179

180

181

182

183

184

185

186

187

188

189

190

191

5-57-67645-200

192
193
194
195
196
197
198
199
200
201
202
203
204
205
206
207

5-57-67645-200

222 Wll
223 Wll
224 Wll
225 Wll
226 Wll
227 Wll
228 Wll
229 Wll
230 Wll
231 Wll

5-57-67645-200

245 Lm

246 Rd

247 Lm

248 Rd

249 Lm
250 Lm*
251 Lm
Fine.
252 Rd*
D.C. al Fine.
253

254 Wll
255 Lm*
256 Wll
257 Wll
258 Cl*

259 Cl*
Fine
D.C. al Fine
260 Rd

261 Cl*
262 Hs*
263 Rd
1.
2.
2.
1.
2.

MELODIA - BOOK III

SIXTH SERIES

Two-part exercises embodying all intervals treated in Series V — More elaborate development of rhythmical difficulties, especially of syncopation — Lengthy solfeggi from German, French, and English sources — Canon and Fugue

6 Bn*
7 Bn
8 Wn
9 Wn
10 Lw
11 Kb*
1.
2.

12 Hg
13 Du*
14 Wn
15 Ts

16 Wn
17 Wn
18 Wn
19 Wn
20 Wn *
21 Wn

22 Wn

23 Wn

24 Wn

25 Wn

26 Wn*

27 Wn
28 Wn
29 Wn*
30 Wn*
31 Wn*

32 Fi

33Fi

34 Sb

35 Sb*

5-57-62645-200

42 Lo*
43

44 Hg
45 Na
46 Hd*

47 Wb
48 Du

49 Du
50 Du*

51 Wb*

52 Wb*

53 Wb
54 St*
55 Hg*

56 Wb
57 Na

58 Wb
59 Wn
60 W11
61 W11

62 Bt
63

64 Pa
65 Pa

66

67 Sn – W11
68 Sb – W11
69 Sb – W11
70 Sb – W11

71 Pa*

72 Pa*

73 Pa

74 Pa*

5-57-67645-200

Hereafter the modern method of cancellation of double-flats and double-sharps — by a single character, omitting the ♮ — will be used.

5-57-67645-200

82

83

84
85
86
3
3

87 Mi Canon for two voices
A
B
88 Mi Canon for two voices
A
B
89 Mi Canon for two voices
A
B

90 *Fugue for two voices*

SEVENTH SERIES

One-part exercises — Systematic treatment of skips to, from, and between chromatic tones — Introductory study of passages whose chromatics "deny" the signature — Advanced solfeggi from foreign sources — Specimen difficulties, without text, from the classics

5-57-67645-200

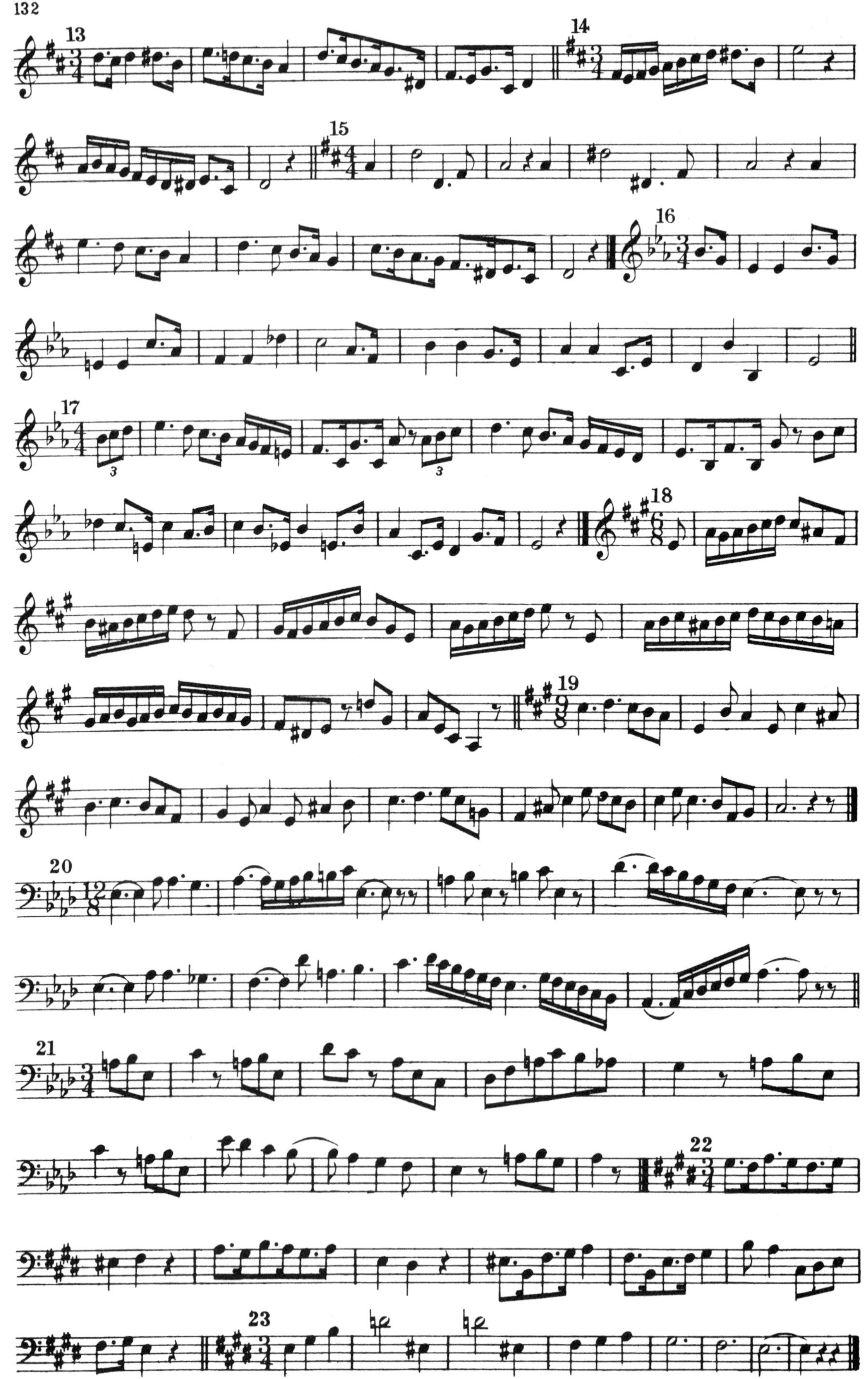
13
14
15
16
17
18
19
20
21
22
23

24

25

26

27

1

2

28

29

30

31

32

Б-57-67645-200

33

34

35

36

37

38

39

40

41
42
43
44
45
46
47
48
49

5-57-67645-200

57
58
59
60
61

62 La*
63 Hd
64 W11
65 W11
66 W11

67 La

68 W11

69 W11

70 W11

71 W11

72 W11

73 W11
74 W11
75 W11
76 W11
77 W11
78 W11

79 W11
80 W11
81 W11
82 Hd*

83 Lm
84 Lm
85Lm
1.
2.
86 Lm

87 Lm
88 Lm
1.
2.
89 Bh
90 Bh
91 Bh*

5-57-67645-200

94

95

96

97

98

99

100

101

102

103

104

105

106

5-57-67645-200

107
108
109
110
111
112
113
114
115
116
117

118
119
120
121
122
123
124

125
126
127

128 Bh
129 Br
130 Bh
131 Bh

5-57-67645-200

EIGHTH SERIES

Two-part exercises, involving all the difficulties treated in Series VII, and fully reviewing the rhythmical problems earlier treated —Maximum difficulties of mediated modulation — Special studies in the development of independence of the parts

5-57-67645-200

4
5
6

7

8

9

10
3
3
3

11

12

13
14
15

16

17

18

19
3/4
20
4/4
3

21 Ch*

MELODIA - BOOK IV

NINTH SERIES

One-part exercises — Typical passages from early and recent composers, with text, of difficulty ranging from medium to great — Full exposition of chromatics which "deny" the signature — Arbitrary changes of tonality

7 Gn
Let me but sit co-zy and dry Un-der the trees with my daugh - ter,
And while raft and boat travel by I drink to the folk on the wa - ter!
8 Ck
Let Israel perish never, Let Judah's gods prevail! Ha! ha ha! ha ha! ha ha! ha
ha! In shackles live forever Nor cease your plaintive wail. Ha! ha ha! ha ha! ha ha! ha ha!
9 Fr
When our hearts are op-prest in the midst of our pleasure, And despair
without meas - ure Has fill'd us with dread; Say, where, Say, where
has gladness fled? Say, where, Say, where has gladness fled?
10 Mn
Take all the prophets of Baal, and let not one of them escape you, Bring them down to Kishon's
brook, and there let them be slain.
11 Vd
Not a trespass go un-smit-ten; Nothing
longer shall be hidden, Not a trespass, Not a tres - pass go un - smitten, go un -
smitten, Not a tres-pass, not a tres - pass go un - smit - - - ten.
12 Gn
This rare cup so ten-der-ly cherish'd, This rare cup so ten-der-ly cherish'd, Aye at his
side the king did keep. And ev-'ry time it touch'd his lip,
He wept and thought of her long per - ish'd.
13 Gn
'Gainst the pow'rs of

E-vil our arms as - sailing, 'Gainst the pow'rs of E - vil our arms as - sail - ing, Strongest
earthly might must be un-a-vail - ing Strongest earthly might must be un - a - vail ing!
14 Hn
And the An-gels struck their im-mor-tal harps, and the wonders, the wonders
of the fifth day sung.
15 Hn
And God said: Let the earth bring forth the living creature after his
kind, cattle, and creeping thing, and beast of the earth after his kind.
16 Hn
And God said, Let there be lights in the fir - ma - ment of heav'n To di -
vide the day from the night, And to give light up - on the earth; And let them
be for signs and for seasons and for days and for years He made the stars also.
17 Hn
And God said, Let the wa-ters under the heavens be gath-er - ed to-geth - er un -
to one place And let the dry land appear and it was so. And God called the dry land
earth, and the gathering of waters called He seas, And God saw that it was good.
18 Hn
And God made the firma - ment and di-vi-ded the wa - ters which were un-der the firma -
ment from the waters which were above the firmament, And it was so.
19 Ab
I'll make some de -
lay! I've travell'd far so I in - tend until to-morrow here to stay, until to - morrow here to stay!

20 Rs
Ei - a Ma - ter, fons a - mo - ris, me sen - ti - re vim do - lo - ris fac
ut te - - - cum la - - ge - am.
21 Hd
He trusted in
God that He would de - liver Him; let Him de - liver Him, if He de - light in Him,
if He delight in Him let Him, deliver Him if He delight in Him, if He delight in
Him, if He delight in Him.
22 Hd
And with His stripes we are heal - - - -
- - - - - ed are heal - - - - ed, are heal - - - -
- - - ed are heal - - - - - ed.
23 Rs
A - - - -
- - - - - - - - - men, A - - - - men,
A - - - - men, A - - - men, A - - - - - - - - -
men, in sem pi - ter - na sae - cu - la, a - - - - - - - -
men, a - men, a - men, a - men, a - - - - - - men, a - - - - men.
24 Vd
When thou shalt come in the midst of fire to judge the world, When Thou shalt come
in the midst of fire to judge the world, in the midst of fire to judge, in the midst of
fire to judge, yea, to judge the world, O Lord God, O Lord God, de - liv - er me, O

God, deliver me, O God, deliver me, de - liv - er me from death, death e -
ter - nal in Thy day of Judg - ment.
25 Fr
I gath - er in each soul im -
mor - tal, Death's dark angel. I. Widely opens Heav'n's flaming portal. See the throne on
high! And which of you, — frail sons ter - restrial, But which of you Can view undis -
may'd God enthron'd in light ce - les - tial, All His might dis - play'd?
26 Fr
Only the meek and childlike soul, Pure in heart and humble in spirit, pure in
heart and humble in spirit, May en - ter this bright, — ho - ly place.
27 Hn
But press'd by ardour now he runs, But press'd by ardour now he runs, Nor
heeds the call, and chiding voice, Nor heeds the call and chiding voice. Then scenting, then
scent - ing the game, He sud - den stops.
28 Hd
Thy rebuke hath broken his heart,
He is full of heaviness, He is full of heaviness, Thy rebuke hath
broken his heart. He look - ed for some to have pity on Him, but there was no
man: niether found He any to comfort Him. He looked for some to have
pity on Him, but there was no man, niether found He any to com - fort Him.

29 Gn
Lo! his Empire is un-dy-ing, Pope and Po-et join the ring, Laurell'd
chiefs his tri-umph sing, Dancing round his pe-des-tal.
30 Hn
Now swarms the vil-lage o'er the mead, The rus-tic youth, the rud-dy
maid: The breathing harvest spreads around, Whose fragrance scents the air; From dale to dale making the
breeze, Resounds the voice of happy labor, Of jo-cund mirth and so-cial glee.
31 Vd
... e - - - le - i - son, chri - - - ste e - le - - i -
son, chri - ste e - le - i - son, e - le - i - son, e - le - i - son.
32 Fr
All the wealth of the earth Is our de-sire, is our de-sire, is our de-sire.
33 Hn
And onward as he bravely toils, In deep-er er-ror plunges still, In
deeper er-ror plunges still, In deep-er er-ror plunges still. De-
press'd his courage sinks, And an-guish fills his heart.
34Fr
The earth is dark, Heav'n's light has faded, Shedding no bright
ray; Ev-'ry hope, ev-'ry hope with sor-row shaded.
35 Hn
Direct us in Thy
ways, O God! O God! Support us in the strife, support us in the strife, O God!

36 Fr
And as of yore, And as of yore See us kneeling, trembling, a - dor - ing,
trembling, a - doring, Bow down once more.
37 Gn
And I, the
frail - est of the frail, Have most need of your for - giveness!
38 Fr
The gods our off'rings
spurning, Scorn each bit - ter cry; To souls all dark with doubts dis - maying, To
souls all dark with doubts dis - maying, O blessed Truth, light re - veal, O blessed Truth!
39 Ad
The skipper he blew a whiff from his pipe, the skipper he blew a
whiff from his pipe, the skipper he blew a whiff from his pipe And a scorn-ful laugh laughed
he, And a scornful laugh laughed he, And a scorn-ful laugh laughed he
40 Mn
Is not his word like a fire? And like a ham-mer that break - eth the
rock? A ham-mer that breaketh the rock, that breaketh the rock in-to pieces? Like a
fire, like a fire, and like a ham - mer that break - eth, that break - eth the
rock. His word is like a fire and like a ham - mer, A ham - mer that
breaketh the rock. For God is an - gry, an-gry with the wick-ed ev-'ry
day; For God is angry with the wicked ev-'ry day, And if the wicked turn not, The

Lord will whet His sword, will whet His sword; and He hath bent his bow, and
made it ready, and made it ready, ready, Is not His word like a
fire? and like a hammer that breaketh the rock, and like a hammer that breaketh the
rock? Is not His word like a fire, and like a ham - mer, a ham - mer that
break - eth the rock? That break - eth the rock, that break-eth the rock; and like a
fire like a ham - mer that break-eth the rock; is not His word like a
hammer that break — eth the rock, is not His word like a hammer that breaketh
— the rock in - to pie - ces? — Is not His word like a ham - mer that
breaketh the rock?
41 Vd
Grace on whom thou wilt be - stowing Save me Lord with mercy
flowing, with mercy flowing! Save me, Lord, save me, Lord, save — me, — Lord!
42 Gn
What wealth is here, what wealth out-bidding gold, Of peace and love, and innocence untold!
What wealth is here, — of peace and love, what wealth out - bidding gold!
43 Ck
'Tis a Jewish woman taken in the vale, And she is passing fair!
She is fair? 'Tis well! Let her approach! Fair Jewish women may my mer - cy gain!

44 Vd
Day of an - ger, Day of an - ger, Day of trouble, Time shall
per - ish, per - ish like a bubble, Day of an - ger, Day of trouble, Time shall
perish like a bubble, So spake David and the Sibyl.
45 Vd
When thou shalt
come in the midst of fire to judge the whole world, in the midst of
fire to judge the whole world.
46 Ck
A - las! A -
las! Thou might'st have saved our lives! A las! our children, our
children and our wives! But now no hope! All hope is gone! But
now no hope! all hope is gone, The blaz - ing sky no pitying raindrop sheds!
47 Bh*
How swiftly the flames of a wrath, all-compel - ling, Rise forth from a heart where God's
love hath no dwelling, And man's dearest treas - - - - - - - - - - - - -
- ure to ru - in is hurl'd. To fix the af - fec - tion on wealth in pro - fu - sion Is
but a de - lu - sion! Take heed, sin - ful world, Is but a de - lu - sion, Is
but a de - lu - sion, Is but a de - lu - sion! Take heed, sin - ful world! Take
heed, sinful world, take heed, sinful world!

48 Bh*
'Tis he, 'tis he, 'tis he who all a - lone, 'tis he who all a -
lone, a - lone, who
all a - lone,
alone hath trod-den the winepress, all alone hath trodden the winepress, a - lone, yea, all a -
lone,
all a - lone, all a - lone, to save
us, erring mor - tals, by cost-ly sac-ri - fice, to save us, err-ing
mortals, by cost-ly sac-ri - fice. Ye Prin - - - - ces, ye Prin - -
- ces, now be-stir ye crown him Lord of all! Ye princes now bestir ye, crown him
Lord of all, crown him Lord of all! Ye Princes, now be -
stir ye, and crown him Lord of all, and crown him Lord of all! Ye Prin - - - -
- ces, now be - stir ye, crown him Lord, O crown him
Lord! Ye Prin - - - - - - - - - - - - - ces, now be -
stir ye, crown him Lord, O crown him Lord of all!

49 Bh*
In vis - - ion I be- - hold, In vis - - - - ion I be -
hold how he, at God's right hand, with lightnings, smites the foe, how he, at God's right hand, with lightnings smites the
foe! In vis - - - - ion I be - hold, in vis - - - - - ion I be -
hold, how he, at God's right hand, with lightnings smites the
foe, to free his faith - ful peo -
ple from wast - ing care and woe, from wast - ing care and woe,
to free his faithful peo - ple from wast - - - - - ing care and woe. I
stand here by the way, and lift my yearn - ing eyes. O
Lord in heav'n a - bove re - ceive my sac - - - - - - - - - -
- - - ri - - fice!
50 Be
In - car - nate fiend, what willst thou now?
What is thy plan, what is thy plan of dire de - struction?
51Ck
Not as the Con-queror comes, They the true hearted came, Not with the roll of the
stirring drums And the trumpet that sings of fame; Not as the fly - ing come in si - lence and in
fear, They shook the gloom with their hymns of loft - y cheer.

52 Rs
Dum pen - de - bat Fi - li - us, dum pen - de - bat. dum pe - de - bat, dum pen-
de - bat Fi - li - us.
53 Ck
They have left unstain'd what there they found Free-
- dom to worship God, to wor - ship God, wor - ship God, to wor - ship, to
wor - ship God, to wor - - - - - - ship God.
54 Py
Mu - sic the fierc-
- est grief can charm, And fate's se - ver - est rage disarm. Music can sof - ten pain to ease,
And make despair and mad - ness please.
Our joys be - low it can im-
prove, And an - te - date our bliss a - bove, and an - - te - date our bliss a - bove.
55 Bh*
At a ges - ture of his fin - ger, man's de - vi - ces halt and fail. At
a gesture of his fin - ger, man's de - vi - ces halt and fail Pow'r and
pride can - not a - vail, pride cannot a - vail. Speaks th' Almight - y but a word, speaks th Almight - y but a word, All His
foes in rage, must vanish, Ye that have His message heard, Forthwith, forthwith, forthwith ev - 'ry world - ly longing ban - - ish. Speaks th' Almight - y but a word, speaks th' Almighty but a word, but a word All his

foes, in rage, must van - ish. Ye who have His message heard, Ye
who have His message heard, Ev - 'ry worldly longing ban - ish.
56 Bh*
De - po - - - - - - su - it, de - po - - - - - - - - - - - su - it, po -
ten - - - - - tes de se - - - - - - - de et ex - al - ta - - - -
- - - - - - - - - - - - - - - - - - - vit hu - mi -
les. De - po - - - - - - - - - su - it, de - po - - - - - - -
- su - it po - ten - - - - - - - tes de se - - - - - - - - de et
ex - al - ta - - - - - - - - - - - - - - - - vit, et - ex - al -
tavit humi - les, ___ et ex - al - ta - - - - - - - - - - vit hu - mi - les.
57 Wg
Thro' waves that rage, and winds that blus - ter, O - ver the wat - 'ry waste I rove; What
respite? That I cannot tell thee, Scarce do I count how seasons move. I can - not name,
name, Shouldst thou de - mand it. The man - y seas I've wander'd o'er: The shore a -
lone my heart doth long for, Ne'er shall I reach, my na - tive shore! The shore a -
lone my heart doth long for, Ne'er shall I reach, my na - tive shore!

58 Wg
Out from the depth of darkness gazing upward, Sore have I long'd a love like hers to
gain; A beating heart was left me, for my torment, That I might still a -
wake to all my pain! This quenchless flame I feel within me burn - ing,
Can I, un - happy one, love dare to call it? Ah no! It is but longing for re - lease,
That I thro' such an angel might have peace, that I thro' such an angel might have peace!
59 Wg
A store of rarest treasures shalt thou see, pearls rich and cost - ly,
stones beyond com - pare. Be - hold, and so con - vince thyself how
great is their val - ue. All these for a friend - ly roof I give thee.
60 Wg
Thee I be - seech, Kind angel sent from heav - en, Thou, who for me didst
win un - look'd for grace, Was there a fruitless hope to mock me giv - en, When thou didst
show me how to find re - lease? Thee I be - seech, Kind an - gel sent from heaven,
Thou who for me didst win un - look'd for grace; Was there a fruit - less
hope to mock me giv - en, When thou didst show me how to find re - lease?
61 Wg
If vain desires and earthly longing Have turn'd my heart from thee a - way,

The sin-ful hopes within me thronging, Be - fore thy blessed feet I lay; I'll

wrestle with the love I cherish'd, Until in death its flame hath perished.

62 Wg

Nay, thou art rav - ing! Tem - per wrath with meas - ure! And I will

teach thee vengeance, God - like pleasure.

63 Wg

For dread re - venge

here I im - plore ye, O Pow'rs that rule our earthly lot, ____ Ye who now

dream of joys be - fore ye, Know that our vengeance slumbers not! Ye who now

dream of joys be - fore ye, Know that our vengeance slum - bers not!

64 Wg

Give heed, O King! In fight I may not lead them! The Grail's sworn champion,

if to mortals known, Must bide its laws, and in obedience heed them; Or ev-'ry pow'r of

manhood he'd dis - own!

65 Bh*

Lau - da - - - mus te, be - ne -

di - ci - mus te, a - do - ra - mus te, glo-ri-fi-ca-mus te, glo - ri - fi - ca - - -

- - - - mus te, glo - ri - fi - ca mus te, a - do - ra - mus te, glo - ri - fi -

- ca - - - - - mus te, glo - ri - fi - ca - mus te, glo - ri - fi - ca - - - - -

- - - - - - - - - - - - - mus te, lau - da - - - - - - - -

- - - - - - - - - mus te, lau - da - mus te, lau -
da - - - - mus te, lau - da - - - - muste ben-e - di-ci-mus te, ado-ra-mus te, glo -
ri - fi-ca-mus te, lau - damus te, benedicimus te, a - - - - - do-ra - mus, glo -
66 Wg
ri - fi - ca-mus te. Truthful runes tomake treaties ri - gid set Wotan
on the shaft of his spear: this served him to sway the world. One bold and
strong destroyed in battle that spear. The binding witness of bonds was shiver'd to
shreds. Then straight Wotan warriors summoned, the world's ashtree's with - er - ing
arms with its stem to splin - ter and sunder. The ash des - troyed. For -
ev - er the spring must go dry. Now round the keen edged stone I
knot the string: Sing, O sister! thou weave it now, Weenst thou why this was?
67 Wg
Westward surg-es slip, eastward speeds the ship. The wind so wild blows homeward now; my
Irish child, where wait - est thou? Say must our sails be weight - ed?
Filled by thy sighs un - bat - ed? Waft us, wind strong and wild! Woe, ah
woe for my child! O Irish maid! my winsome, mar - vellous maid!

TENTH SERIES

Two part exercises, with text — Representative excerpts from early and recent composers, with a few new exercises, embodying maximum difficulties of pitch and rhythm, as well as the utmost independence of parts

4 Hd
men, a - men, For we turn
men, a - men. For we turn
ed ev-'ry one to his own way.
ed, for we turn ed.
5 Hd
But thou com-fortest my heart in its op-pres
But thou comfortest my heart in its op-pres
sion, its op-pres
sion, its op-pres
sion.
6 Bh
A
sion. Praise and hon-or and glo-ry and pow'r be
men. Praise and hon-or and glo-ry and
un-to God for-ev-er and for-ev ermore. A
pow'r be un-to God for - ev-er and for-ev - er-more!
men.

7 Hd
Age un-to age telleth forth all the wonders of thy glo - - - - - -
Age un-to age telleth forth all the wonders of thy glo - - - - - -
- ry, and re - joic - - - - - - - eth in thy might.
- - ry; and re - joic - - - - - -eth in thy
Age un-to age tell-eth forth all the wonders of thy glo - - - - - -
might, and re-joic - - eth in thy might, in thy might,
- - - - - - - - - - - - - - - ry, and re-joic - -
re-joic - - eth, re-joic - - eth in thy might,
- - - - - - - - - eth in thy might, and re -
and re-joic - - - - eth, and re-joic - - - - - eth in thy might.
joic - - eth, and re - joic - - - - - - - - - eth in thy might.
8 Bh
There is neither speech nor language, there is nei-ther speech nor lan - - - -
Nei - - - - - - - - - - - - - - ther, nei - - - -

guage, there is nei - ther speech nor lan -
ther speech nor lan - guage, there is nei - ther speech nor
guage, their voice
language, there is nei - ther speech nor lan - guage their voice can
cannot be heard.
9 Hd
The dove
not cannot be heard. Pin - ing,
as he flut - ters, his plaint soft - ly
long - ing, his
ut - ters; he's cal - ling, he's
plaint gen - tly ut - ters; he's cal - ling his lov'd one, The
cal - ling his lov'd one. The dove. as he flut - ters his
dove. as he flut - ters, his
plaint
plaint soft - ly ut - ters, he's cal - ling, he's

soft-ly ut-ters he's cal-ling
cal- ling his lov'd one, he's cal-ling
10 Hd
his lov'd one.
Love now u-nit
his lov'd one.
Love now u-nit
eth a hap-
eth, Love now u-nit-
py pair hap- py pair.
Love now u-nit-
eth a hap- py pair,
Love now u-nit- eth, Love
eth, Love now u-nit- eth, u-nit-eth,
Love now u-
now u-nit-eth, Love now u-nit- eth, u-nit-eth.
nit-
Love now u-nit- eth Love now u-
eth a hap- py pair.
nit- eth a hap- py pair.

11 Mz
Chri-ste e-le- - - - - - - - - - - -
Ky - ri - e e - le - - i - son, e - le - - - - - - - -
- i - son, Ky - ri - e e - le - i - son, e - le - - - -
- - - - - - - i - son, e - le - i - son, Christe e - le - - - - - - - - -
- - - - - - - - - - - -i - son, e - le - i - son.
- - - - - - - - - - - - -i - son, e - le - - - i - son.
12 Be *
In glo - - - -
In glo - - - - - - - - ri-a Dei pa - tris, a - - - men, a -
- - - - ri-a Dei, a - - - men.
- - men a - - - - - - - men
13 Bh
Ky-ri-e e-le - - -
Ky - ri - e e - le - - - - - - -
- - - - - - i - son, Ky - ri - e e - le - - - i - son, e -
- - - - i son, Ky - ri - e e - le - i - son, e - le - i - son.
le - - - - - - - - - - - i - son, e - le - - - - - - - - i - son.

14 Bh*
Ky-ri - e elei - - - - son,ele - i -
Ky-ri-e e - lei - son, e - le-i-son, e - - - - le - i - son, Ky - - ri-
son, e - - - - - le - i - son, e - - - - - - le - i - son
e e-le- - - - - - i - son, e - le - - - - - - - - - i - son
15 Bh
Cum sancto Spi - - ri-tu in glo- - - - - - - - - - - - - - - -
Cum sancto spi - ri-tu in glo- - - - -
- ria Dei Patris,A-men, a- - - - - - - - - - - - - - -
- - - - - - - ria Dei Patris A-men a- - - - - - - - - men
- men
16 Bh*
Chri-ste e-le- - - - - - i-son,ele- - - - - - - - - - - - -
Chri-ste e-le- - - - i - son,elei- - - - - - - - - - - -
i-son, Chri - ste, Christe,e-le - - - i-son,ele- - - - - - - - -
- son,Chri-ste,Christe e-le- - - - - i-son,ele- - - - - - - - - - - -

i-son, e-le- i - son, e-le- i - son,Christe e-le- i - son.
- i-son, e-le - i - son, e-le - i - son,Christe ele - i - son,Christe ele - - -
Christe e-le - - i-son,e - le-i-son, ele - i - son, e-le - i-son,Chri-
- i-son, e - le-i-son, e - le - i - son,e-le - - i-son,Christe ele - - i-son,Christe e-le- -
te ele - i-son,Christe ele - - - - - - - i-son,Christe ele - - i-son,e-
- - - - i-son,Christe e - - - - - - - - - i-son,Christe e-
le- i - son, e - le - - - i-son, Chri - ste, Chri-ste,e-le - - - -
le - i - son, e - le - - - i-son, Chri - ste, Chri-ste,e-le - - - -
- - - - - - - - - i-son,Christe e-le - - - - - - i- son, e-
- - - - - - - - - - i-son Christe e - le - - - i - son, e-
le - - i-son, e-le - - - - - i-son,Christe e - le - i - son.
le - i - son,e-le - - - - - i-son,Christe e - le - i - son.
17 Bh
Do - mi-ne De-us,a-gnus Dé - i, Do - mine De-us, agnus De - - i,
Do - mine De-us,a-gnus De - i, Do-mi-ne De - - - us,agnus De - i,

a - gnus De - i, Fi -li-us Pa - tris, Domine De-us,agnus De-i. agnus Dei. Domine
a - gnus De - i, Fi - li-us Pa - tris, Domine De-us,agnus De-i, agnusDei, Domine
De-us, a - gnus De - - - - i, Fi - li - us Pa - - - - tris.
De-us, a - gnus De - i, Fi - li -us Pa - - - - - - - - tris.
18 Bh
Et ex Patre ex Patre na - - tum, et ex Patre, ex Patre na - tum ante
Et ex Patre, ex Patre, na - - - tum et ex Patre, ex Patre, na - -
o - - - - - - - - mnia Sae - - - - -cula, an-te omnia saecula.
- tum, ante o - - - - - - - - -minia sae - - - - - - - - cu - la.
19
To battle haste, to battle haste,O haste! The foe lurketh nigh!
To battle. to battle, O haste! The foe lurk - eth nigh.
Smite him to earth, yea, smite him to earth!
Smite him, smite him, smite him, yea, smite him to
To battle haste, to battle haste, O haste! The foe,the foe, lurk-eth,
earth! To battle haste, to battle haste, haste! The

20 Fr
— lurk - eth nigh! — Now, as of yore, now, as of yore, Thy people
foe lurketh, lurketh nigh! Now as of yore, now as of yore,
trembling and a - dor - ing, Bow — down once more —
Thy people, trembling and a - doring, Bow down once more —
21 Fr *
Our sacrifices spurn - ing, Silent to our cry, Our sac - ri - fi - ces
Our sacri-fi-ces spurn - ing, Silent to our cry, Our sac-ri - fi-ces spurn - ing,
spurn - ing, Silent to our cry, Ye gods, to us in darkness lying, ye
Silent to our cry, ye gods, to us in darkness lying, ye gods, to
gods, to us in darkness lying, send the light, the bless - èd truth.
us in darkness lying, O send the light, — send the light, the bless - èd truth.
22 Cb
Dream of de - light, — en - kind - ling the soul, O why canst thou
Dream of de-light, en - kindling the soul, — O why canst thou not
— not ling - er? Thou hov'rest a - bove Like a flut - ter - ing dove!
ling - er? Thou hov'rest a - bove Like a flut - ter - ing dove!

Vision of heav'n, O stay! Shed en - tranc - ing radiance
Vision of heav'n, O stay! Shed en - tranc - ing radiance
as of end-less day! Like a dove Like a dove
as of endless day! hov'rest thou,
Ah! Dream of de light, en - kindling the soul,
hov'rest thou, Dream of de - light, en - kind - ling the
O, why canst thou not ling - - - er? Thou hov - rest
soul, O, why canst thou not ling - er? Thou hov'rest a - bove
23 Cn
like a dove! Ac-cur-sèd Ca-di,
like a dove! Ac - cur - sèd Ca-di, who, cold-hearted, A
ac-cur-sed Ca - di, A guest with - in thy house didst
guest with - in thy house didst slay, 'Tis time that
slay, Ac-cur-sèd Ca-di, thou di-est to - day!
thou and life were part-ed; Thou di - est to - day!

24
Hear thy children, Lord, hear their pe - ti - tion!
We hope, O Lord, in thee, we hope, we hope, Lord we hope, O
With richest boun - ty hast thou blessed thy faith - ful people!
Lord in thee. With bounty hast thou blessed thy faith - ful people! We
Hear thy children, O heed their pe - ti - tion! We hope,
hope, O Lord in thee, we hope, we hope, O Lord, in thee, we
we hope, O Lord, in thee!
25
Sail a - way, sail a - way,
hope in thee!
Now to the east, now to the
have no care of the morrow.
O wind, blow
west, All is one to the men of the sea. Storm beat, and wind, blow!
blow! We de - fy ye!
26
Swift ad-vancing,
Storm beat, and wind, blow! We de-fy ye! Swift ad -van - cing,
ban-ners streaming, sa - bres gleaming, coursers prancing, comes the foe!
ban - ners streaming, sa - bres gleaming, coursers prancing, comes the foe!

27

Ho! ye chieftains, ye I scorn! Ho! ye chieftains, ye I scorn!

Nay, nay, they dare not, nay, they dare not heed the call! Nay, nay, they dare not heed the

Hide not in dread, cowards all! Here be - hold me ready! Hide not, -

call! Hide not in dread. Our champion waits! Hide not in dread, our champion waits!

— cow - ards all!

28

Who hath strength to win the

Come, ye cowards all! Who hath strength to win the

bat - - tle? Who ah! who can quell, quell the strife?

bat - - - - tle? Who. ah! who can quell the strife? Who

Who can quell the strife?

29

What ho! what ho! Let the port-cul - lis

can quell, can quell the strife? Let the port - cul - - lis

fall! He shall not, he shall not es - cape us now!

30

Far from the

fall! He shall not es - cape us now! Far

mad - ding crowd's ig - no - ble strife, Their so - ber

far, far from the madding crowd

wish - es ne - ver learn'd to stray, to stray. Far
Their so - ber wish - es ne - ver learn'd to stray
from the madding crowds ig - no - ble strife Their so - ber
Far, far, far from the madding crowd
wish - es, Their so - ber wishes ne - ver learn'd to stray,
Their so - ber wish - es ne - ver learn'd to stray,
never learn'd to stray. Press on, press on, ye
never learn'd to stray, learn'd to stray. Press on, press on, ye
31
sons of light, press on, press on, Un - tir - ing in your no - ble
sons of light, Un - tir - ing in your no - ble
fight; Still tread - ing each new foeman down, each foe - man down,
fight, Still tread - ing each new foe - man, each foe - man down, And
And battling for a bright - - - er, a bright - er crown!
batt - ling for a bright-er crown, a bright - er crown!

ELEVENTH SERIES

Two-part exercises, partly without and partly with text, in the following Church Modes: Aeolian, Dorian, Ionian, Mixolydian, Phrygian — Canonic imitation, strict and free, in other intervals than that of the octave

3 *Ionian* — Bt

4 *Dorian* — Bt

5 Dorian — Bt
6 Mixolydian — Bt

7 Aeolian —Bt

8 La

9 Phrygian —Bt

10 Mixolydian Ls
Be - - - ne-di - ctus. qui ve - - - - - -
Be - - - - ne - di - ctus, qui
- - - - - nit in no-mi - ne Do - - - -
ve - - - - nit in no-mi-ne Do - - - - - - - - - - - - -
- - - - - mi - ni, in no-mi - ne, in no-mi - ne.
- - - - mi - ni, in no-mi - ne in no-mi - ne
in no-mi - ne Do - - - - - - mi - ni.
in no-mi - ne Do - - - - - - - - - - mi - ni.
11 Mixolydian Ls Wll
Ex - pan - di ma-nus me - - - - as
Ex-pan - di ma-nus me - - - - as ad te:
ad te: a - ni-ma me - a a - ni-ma me - a si - cut ter -
a-ni-ma me - a a - ni-ma me - a si-cut ter - ra si - -
- ra si - ne a - - - qua ti - - - - - - - - bi
- ne a-qua ti - bi si - ne a - qua ti - - - - - bi.

12 Mixolydian Ls
Be - ne - di - ctus, qui ______ ve - nit in no - - mi - ne Do - - - - - - - mi - ni, ______ in no - mi - ne, in no - - mi - ne, in no - mi - ne, in no - mi - ne Do - - - mi - ni.
Be - ne - di - ctus, qui ______ ve - nit in no - mi - ne Do - - mi - ni in no - - - - mi - ne. Do - - - mi - ni, in no - - mi - ne Do - mi - ni, in no - mi - ne, in no - mi - ne. Do - - - mi - ni.
13 Mixolydian Ls
Do - mi - ne De - us, Do - mi - ne De - us Do - mi - ne De - us, A - gnus De - i, A - gnus De - - i, Agnus De - i. Fi - li - us Pa - tris, Fi - li - us Pa - tris Fi - li - us Pa - tris. Fi - li - us Pa - - - - - - - - tris.
Do - mi - ne De - us, Do - mi - ne De - us, Do - mi - ne De - us, A - gnus De - i, A - gnus De - i, Fi - li - us Pa - tris, Fi - li - us Pa - - - - tris Fi - li - us Pa - tris Fi - li - us Pa - - - - - - - tris.

14 Ionian Hn
Cru-ci-fi-xus e-ti-am pro no - - bis, sub Pon-ti - o Pi - la - -
Cru - ci - fi - xus e - ti - am pro no - bis, sub Ponti - o Pi-la-
to pas-sus et se-pultus est. Et re-sur-re - xit ter-ti-a di - e secundum
to pas-sus et sepul-tus est. Et re-sur-re - xit ter-ti-a di - e
scri - ptu - ras. Et ascen-dit et ascen-dit in coe - - - lum se-
se-cundum scriptu - ras. Et ascen - dit, et ascen - dit in coe - lum,
- det ad de - xteram Pa - - - - - tris
se - dit ad de - xte-ram Pa - - - tris
15 Phrygian Ls
Auditu-
Audi-tu-i me-
i me - - o da - - - - - bis gau - - di - um et
o da - - bis gau - di - um et
laeti - - - ti - am: et e-xul-ta-bunt et e-xul-ta -
laeti - - ti - am: et e-xal - ta-bunt os - sa
bunt os - sa hu - mi - li - a - ta, os - sa hu-mi-li - a -
humi - li - a - - - - ta, humi - li-a - ta, os - sa hu -

End of Melodia

PRESSER ESSENTIALS for Voice

METHODS

CLIPPINGER
Class Method of Voice Culture (431-40089)

COLE & LEWIS
Melodia – A Course in Sightsinging
Book One (431-40073)
Book Two (431-40074)
Complete, Books I-IV (431-40077)

COLLECTIONS

ART SONGS FOR SCHOOL AND STUDIO *(ed. Glenn & Spouse)*
1st Year, Medium High (431-40092)
1st Year, Medium Low (431-40093)
2nd Year, Medium High (431-40094)
2nd Year, Medium Low (431-40095)

CLASSIC ITALIAN SONGS *(ed. Glenn & Taylor)*
Volume One, Medium High (431-40102)
Volume One, Medium Low (431-40103)

FRENCH ART SONGS *(ed. Glenn & Taylor)*
Medium High(431-40109)
Medium Low (431-40110)

SOLOS

BONDS, MARGARET
He's Got the Whole World In His Hands (151-00360)

DUNGAN, OLIVE
Eternal Life
Low in B♭ (121-40002)
High in D (121-40009)

DVORAK/FISHER
Goin' Home
High (131-40284)
Medium (131-40285)
Low(131-40286)

DUETS

Choice Sacred Duets(431-40070)
Sacred Duets *(ed. Shakespeare)*
Volume One - 2 High Voices(421-40000)
Volume Two - High & Low Voices (421-40001)

LITERATURE

ELSON, LOUIS
Elson's Pocket Dictionary (437-40027)

OREM, PRESTON WARE
Harmony Book for Beginners(417-40040)